Leslie,

Thanks for sharing yourself with us and welcoming us to the community. I appreciate the opportunity to share this piece of my soul with you.

With love and appreciation,

Rick

6-19-01

The Tao of
Beach Glass

Rick McCabe

published by Jackie & Rick McCabe

www.beachglassmoments.com

Author and photographer: Rick McCabe
Cover art and design: Rima McCabe
Photo selection and sequencing: Rima McCabe
Page layout and design: Deb Citron-Stevens
Editing and production: Jackie McCabe
Print manager: Joseph Profetto

Jackie & Rick McCabe

P.O. Box 1600, Gloucester, MA 01931

ISBN 0-9657553-1-2

Dedicated with love and appreciation to my brother
Robert Leo Grossman
who is blazing the path on the other side of the veil.

RJM

Acknowledgments

This book owes its existence to many people (and one dog) but primarily to three who made very direct contributions.

Roxie was truly my partner on each step reported on in this journey. She is the one that got me out on the beach each morning and led more than followed on the path.

My wife Jackie is my partner at so many levels and in so many ways. Not only did she introduce me to beach glass but to dimensions of myself and life not previously experienced.

My daughter Rima was the creative mid-wife of this project making numerous contributions. She has the soul of an artist and lent that soul to me for the purpose of producing this book. It is she that nagged me to take pictures on the beach for months, holding the vision of what was possible. She reviewed, selected and sequenced those photos. Rima did all of the initial layouts and design work for the entire book. Whatever you see here graphically, started with her vision.

I said three and should stop there before acknowledgments outweigh the text of the book. But, without two additional acknowledgments to the foundation of this project, I would be remiss.

Ken Fleming, in sharing the process of his writing with me, in intimate detail, taught me more about that process and the possibility writing offers than I had ever imagined. His generosity of spirit has been limitless.

Over thirty years ago I walked into the SoHo loft of Harold Feinstein in New York City and met the first great teacher of my life. In a class, ostensibly to teach photography, Harold taught people "how to see" and opened me to a life long exploration of my soul.

To these individuals and to all who contributed to my life and to this book, my profound appreciation.

*W*hy look for beach glass? Or, perhaps more to the point, why write about it. An act so simple and seemingly without value can hardly be worth our attention. Or can it?

The search for God (or whatever the politically correct term for the larger presence than ourselves from which we have come and to which we will return) is presented as a complex, life long task. And yet, at another level, it is quite simple. Meister Eckhart said that the spiritual journey is the shortest journey in the world — a matter of inches. Perhaps that is the lesson we will learn in the analogy of beach glass.

In searching for beach glass there is much to learn that can lead us closer to God, to wisdom, to an understanding of the universe. And it's not just beach glass. It's in all the simple acts and opportunities and gifts that surround us every day of our lives. To most of them we are totally oblivious — or at least most of us are. Beach glass is but one minute paradigm that I invite you to consider and explore through these few words.

If you're not looking for beach glass, you won't find it.

*S*ometimes, when you're not looking, in a place where you would not expect to find beach glass, a beautiful, large piece of beach glass presents itself, and then perhaps another. Then, as you start to look for beach glass, there is no more to be found.

If you ignore the very small, insignificant pieces of beach glass
you will almost certainly miss some "treasures" of beach glass
which remain unseen until the moment in which
you are retrieving the insignificant piece.

A large black dog is a great aid in the search for beach glass. Often, she will lead you to superb pieces of beach glass in spots you would have otherwise missed. And, she'll do this over and over again as a constant lesson in both humility and gratitude.

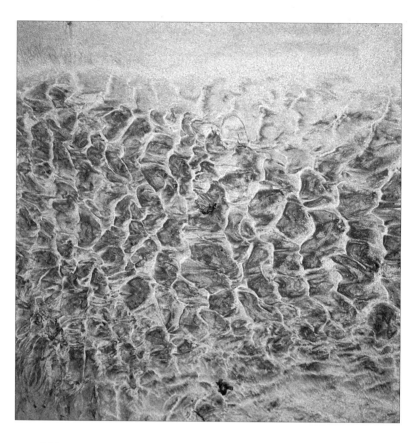

*W*hen conditions on the beach are unusual, look for beach glass in unusual places. The beach glass and the beach are in harmony, working together in a dance that requires both partners. 🐚

Finding beach glass requires the light. The more light, the more beach glass one will find. Beach glass cannot be found in the dark. The dark is a time of preparation.

*T*he path back is very different from the path
on the way out. No matter how thoroughly
you comb the beach on the way out,
you'll find beach glass that remained unseen
until the way back — it's a different path,
lit differently and to be experienced
differently. 🐚

*W*hen looking for beach glass with a partner,
celebrate and feel the joy of each piece of
beach glass found by your partner as if it were
your own and it will be. 🐚

*T*he colder the temperature, the stronger the wind, the deeper your desire to never remove your gloves, the more beach glass you'll find, especially if you're Roman Catholic.

*W*hen you expect to find beach glass in a certain place, in a certain quantity based on whatever conditions you have observed over time, you will be disappointed. It won't be there. One must be free of expectation. 🐚

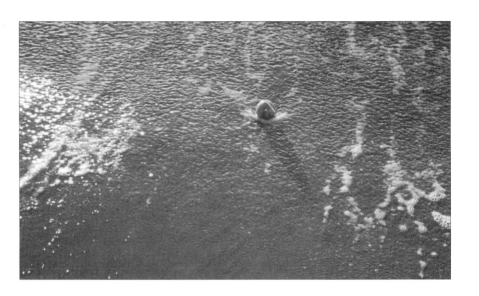

*T*he more joy, the more inward Light you bring to the task,

the more beach glass you will find.

*I*f you live on the beach, collect beach glass.
The ocean will replenish what you find, the source unending,
even when it appears to end. 🐚

*W*hen we give a gift of a bottle of beach glass to friends it appears to be without value and yet is the most treasured gift we could give them.

The sun, prior to its rising, casts an ever increasing amount of light in imperceptible increments. If one looks, beach glass, previously hidden in the darkness will come into view, and then more and more, until the full light of the risen sun is upon us.

A *piece of beach glass is spotted*
and draws us and unknowingly
we'll step over and through
several (maybe many) other
pieces as we follow the fixed focus
of our vision, failing to see the
abundance that our find obscures;
raising the question, in finding
what we find, what are we
obscuring from view.

*T*he day's collection of beach glass, when added to the whole,
reminds us of our place in the universe — very large when focused
on, but almost unseen, yet a critical part of the whole, when viewed
with the entirety. 🐚

*E*ach day I find beach glass I leave it next to the sink for my wife to discover — an unexpected gift and treasure that speaks of my love for her beyond words.

*B*each glass is not found on every

beach just as truth is not found

everywhere. 🐚

Looking for beach glass requires a constant single-minded focus and intense concentration that screens out all distractions. However, occasionally, it is necessary to give up that focus and concentration and give yourself over to the rising sun to record in your heart a moment that will pass quickly and never come again.

*A*s in all of life, there is a hierarchy with beach glass — based on its rarity. On our beach, blue glass is the most valued. We search for the "Great Blue Piece," the Moby Dick of beach glass, assuming that it will bring more happiness than the more "ordinary" pieces. 🐚

*T*he more you reach deep inside

to say what there is to say about beach glass

the less there is to say. It is just beach glass.

*O*ne particular morning, before first light, in the dark, I was gifted
with a piece of beach glass which led me to diligently search for
more. Finding none, I proved the rule that "you can't find beach glass
in the dark" but that doesn't mean that you can't be gifted with what
you were not looking for — even when it's dark.

*W*hile on the beach, never cease looking
for beach glass. You never know when
you'll be gifted. Even when the ocean
is devouring the beach like a hungry bear
devouring honey, be prepared to receive. 🐚

Sometimes you'll walk on the beach and all the places you would normally look for beach glass are occupied by the ocean so you look where you would normally never think to look. You look because you realize the value is in the looking, perhaps more so than in the finding. And you find a plethora of beach glass because you were looking without expectation. Without expectation you can see what you were not able to see before in a place that you never expected would hold what you were looking for. Sit with that lesson for a while.

*S*top, just stand in the midst of the rocks and concentrate. Before long, beach glass previously hidden from view will become obvious, dancing like jewels in the sunlight just waiting for you to quiet yourself and be ready to receive.

*Y*ou can stroll the beach and find a piece of beach glass here and there and you will not even have begun to experience looking for beach glass. Without time, concentration, focus, and commitment you will not begin to learn what beach glass has to teach, reminding us how easy it can be to taste an experience and how much more is required to "own" it. To be taught by it. To be born into it.

*B*each glass is created in a ceaseless dance between the ocean and the beach, each requiring the other for an indeterminable period of time for a purpose of no importance. It's just beach glass.

If gifted with a piece of beach glass, claim it without
hesitation. If it were meant for another, you would not
have seen it. And, just maybe, you are to be the conduit
for that beach glass to another. If such is the case, you'll
know it when the time arrives.

*S*ome mornings you search the beach diligently and don't find
any beach glass but you realize that you've had a wonderful
walk on the beach and that is the gift.

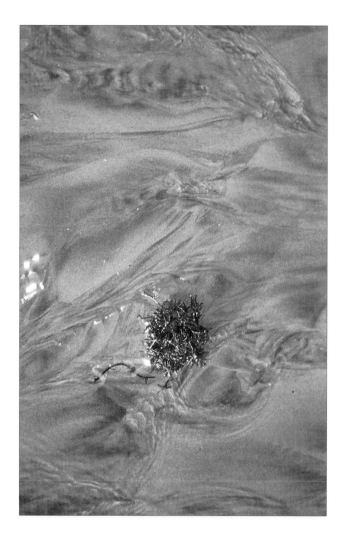

*W*hen pulled off course by something you are certain is a beautiful piece of beach glass, only to discover it is not beach glass at all, don't give in to the disappointment. Instead ask yourself why you have been brought to this place, and often you'll be rewarded with an unexpected gift of beach glass. 🐚

*W*hen you hit stretches of time where you are finding very few pieces of beach glass, it's an opportunity to practice celebrating what you do have. Some mornings the sun rises with a brilliant fanfare of color, a breathtaking display of its grandeur, and other mornings it pops up with nary a peep. On either morning the sun has risen and the day begun. And as with beach glass, each piece becomes part of the whole.

Is beach glass meant to be found? Is life meant to be lived? Does God exist apart from us? Not knowing the answers with certainty, we go forward. 🐚

Sometimes you arrive home to discover that what appeared to be an ordinary piece of beach glass while on the beach is a spectacular and rare blue piece and you wonder how you could have confused this gem with the ordinary, how you could have failed to spot its magnificence. Then, you might realize that that is exactly what we do each day in so many ways. We do that in terms of our own magnificence. 🐚

*S*ometimes you can see a piece of beach glass
a hundred yards off, or so it seems, and other times
you can't see a piece of beach glass when you are
standing right on top of one. I'm certain there is a
lesson in that, I just don't know what it is.

What should I say? That I'm going out to walk the dog.
That I'm going out to get some exercise. That I'm going out to
commune with nature. That I'm going out to write a book about
beach glass. That I'm going out to spend precious time looking
for something of no intrinsic value, beach glass. That I'm going
out to stir my stagnant soul. That I'm going out to search for
God. That I'm going out to learn the lessons that await me
around the next bend. Or, "D," all of the above.

*I also collect special rocks from the beach and
polish them in a lengthy process to bring out their
jewel-like nature. Beach glass is already polished to
a jewel-like nature and, given enough time,
the rocks would be too.* 🐚

The beach rocks are rough and nondescript, but, when polished, become shining jewels — from the action of the grit, tumbling and general wear and tear. It's a process, not unlike life, where in the end, their souls are released to shine in their full glory.

All the effort required to release the soul of the rocks I polish is accomplished without intervention by the beach and the ocean. Yet it is the intervention of the beach and the ocean that produces beach glass. What is the intervention required to birth our soul, or does God accomplish that by divine presence in each of us. And yet, the soul within the rock is present before the intervention or it could not be released. Perhaps that is the way it is with us: the soul is present but requires the process of living to shine — if it is to shine. Not every rock gets polished. 🐚

You can't look for rocks to polish and beach glass at the same time. Each requires its own focal point. If you look for one, you won't see the other even though occasionally a rock shows up when looking for beach glass and vice versa. It's a little like wealth and happiness (or any other pairings that may come to mind). You can't search for both at the same time even though, if they choose, they might show up at the same time.

*W*hat is the source of beach glass? You cannot know with certainty. In part, no doubt, it comes from industrial waste and household garbage dumped in the ocean as well as from teenagers drinking on the beach to hide from the sight of their parents and the police. It's hard to realize that these jewels emanate from such an inglorious beginning. What's the lesson in this? Maybe it is just one more example of the universe's need for balance of the light and the dark. Maybe it's like our attempts to legislate morality and integrity where all we produce is more litigation and lawyers — integrity is now the interpretation of the law and no longer the truth.

Nothing jewel-like about that! 🐚

Is the moment of resurrection for beach glass when it delivers itself to the person finding it in its jewel-like state, or does the moment of resurrection come when it is separated from the whole, or is it when it is formed from sand to glass, or is it when it separates from the rock to begin its journey to sand, or is it when it is ground down to return to sand? Perhaps, like us, its life consists of a never-ending series of resurrections, many of which go unnoticed and uncelebrated, others are lost in a momentary flash of brilliance. 🐚

*Y*ou find a beautiful, jewel-like piece of beach glass. You can
pick it up, put it in your pocket. You hang on to it so that you
can share it with your friends and family, and so you can
reconnect with the experience whenever you wish.
You carry it with you in order to capture the moment of
discovery, and all that went with it, for eternity.
But how do you do that with a sunrise.
And how about with God.

*B*each glass is not sold or purchased, that I know of, because in and
of itself it has no value. All you buy is a piece of glass, you don't get
the joy of finding it, the reminder of the sunrise, the experience of
God or the lesson that is taught by that particular piece of beach
glass. Perhaps this is analogous to why we cannot find or experience
God for another — no matter what anyone says. That's the lesson
from this morning's beach glass which, otherwise, looks quite like
another morning's. But it is so much more.

I receive this morning's offering of beach glass, under the glare of the sunrise, with the same awe and reverence that I receive the body of Christ in the form of the Host at Mass. Is there a difference?

Some mornings you can be so into yourself, in a fog,

that even the sunrise doesn't penetrate or register.

You may still be collecting beach glass but it's for

production — how much, how quickly. You realize

that this experience of collecting beach glass bears

very little resemblance to other mornings. The lesson

is not realized at the time, but it is there. That lesson

is that any activity, even the most sacred, can be

done in a way that removes all its manna. And, if the

universe's need for balance is correct, the corollary

must also be true — the simplest, most humble and

ordinary experience can be a doorway to God.

St. John of the Cross certainly spoke eloquently

(with his life) to that point.

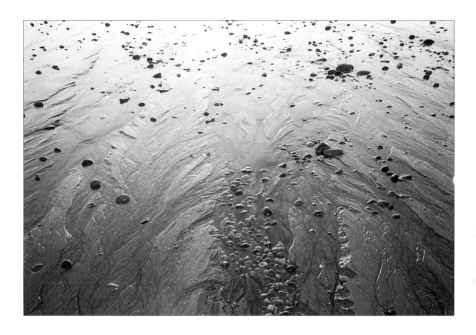

*A*t night I walk on the beach, caressed by the dark, relieved of
finding beach glass, absorbing the lesson(s) of the day. 🐚

If I'm arrested for having my dog on the beach during the summer months when we're legislated off the beach can I claim that she's an integral part of my religious practice and show them a copy of this book as proof — every religion has a sacred text, ergo, if you have a sacred text it must be a religion.

Or, would that denigrate the sacredness of my pursuit. 🐚

*M*ornings where I return from the beach with my
beach glass pocket overflowing with beach glass are no
different from mornings where I return with a couple of
pieces, if I'm into the experience and if, this is a big if,
I have been on the beach as a supplicant,
open to the sacred.

A *piece of beach glass not gathered will not be there the*

next day or even at the next low tide. It may never appear

again, the opportunity to gather it being singular.

Life's opportunities can be like that.

There is nothing to do about that but to

know it, respect it and honor it —

and not to be so cavalier about opportunities. 🐚

*N*ew glass deserves its opportunity to mature and grow into beach glass, and is best left on the beach where it is found so that it might proceed with its process. If you're meant to have it, it will return to you when it's ready. 🐚

Today was a plain vanilla day — or at least, so it seemed.
I woke up feeling blah. The day was gray and dull outside.
There was nothing special or bright as I began my routine.
And today I was gifted with beach glass in quantity, quality,
color (including two rare dark blue pieces) and a lesson:
never stop searching, no matter what the circumstances,
because you can never know when the universe
will choose to bestow its gifts upon you,
gifts you may not even be looking for.

*S*omeone told me that I could use the tumbler in which I polish beach rocks to create beach glass. What would be the point. Beach glass is not about having it, but discovering it and making it your own — the process. There are no lessons in creating your own beach glass. It's like taking someone else's vision of God as your own. How close to God can that put you. If you don't walk through your own valley and climb your own mountains how can you truly know God. 🐚

*P*arsifal searched for the Grail. I search for beach glass. Is
one journey less arduous or less spiritual than the other?
It all depends how the journey is undertaken. Either can be
profane. Either can be sacred. We walk the path that
is provided to us to walk. That is the given.
How we walk it, that is the choice.

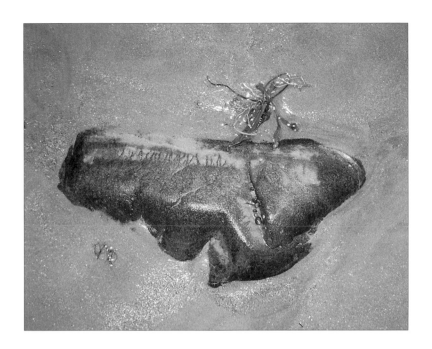

I doubt that there was beach glass in King Arthur's time. There are no dragons in existence today — that I know of. We each have to walk the journey we're given. We can learn from the journeys of others, but, to be seduced into walking them will only keep us from our own journey, and it is only in our own journey that we will arrive to that place life requires of each of us. So, today I collected beach glass and all that goes with it. It didn't seem as important as slaying a dragon when I started.

Some mornings I go out on the beach searching for beach glass
and all I learn are the same lessons over and over again.
And, that is good. It's enough to warm the heart even when
the temperature is in single digits.

A good morning of looking for beach glass, the beach thoroughly combed and my beach glass pocket bulging when Roxie pulls me off the return course to a spot I had already searched. She'd dropped her ball on a large, partly obscured, but readily visible once you'd seen it, piece of beach glass. Synchronicity or coincidence? I don't know. I do know that she keeps doing it over and over again.

*S*ome beach glass retains a part of its former identity — a unique color, shape, remnant of writing . . . making me realize how tenaciously we often hang on to the old parts of our long past identities even when they no longer serve us, and may keep us from being fully who we are now. And, some of those old parts are what make us special now. 🐚

I often write in the collective voice — "we."
I do that to open these lessons to all who might
read them. But, perhaps the greater motivation is
to soften their directness and the urgency
they have in my own life.

There is something seductive about the water's edge at low tide. Even though beach glass is not found there, we often walk that route back, knowing that a few pieces of beach glass will be left unfound. But there is something else we get along the water's edge at low tide that makes the sacrifice worthwhile even if we don't know what it is that we are getting. 🐚

*There are sections of the beach
that I walk where I never find beach
glass. However, I always look.
And, every once in a while a piece
of beach glass gifts itself to me and
I have to reexamine the concept
of never — and all my
pre-conceived notions.*

Coincidence or synchronicity, you tell me. The best rocks for polishing are found on that part of the beach where beach glass is never found. The portion of the beach that contains the most beach glass is virtually devoid of rocks that are good for polishing. Perhaps it's a reminder that we receive the gifts we need where and when we need them. And, occasionally when beach glass is found where you look for rocks, and rocks for polishing where you look for beach glass it is a reminder that our gifts are to be found where we'd never expect to receive them.

This morning, walking on that part of the beach where you never find beach glass . . . except when you do . . . I found a small, insignificant piece just as I concluded my prayer. The context of finding it transformed its insignificance into a magnificence it otherwise did not possess. Was it coincidence or synchronicity that delivered this magnificent gift at that moment, particularly given the grayness of the day — within and without. It does nothing for my heart to treat it as coincidence. It warms my heart and brightens my day to treat it as synchronicity — a gift from God. So that is how I will hold it. It costs me nothing to hold it this way but gives me much. How many gifts from God do I explain away or overlook in my life?

This morning I really "needed" to find beach glass to feel better about myself and about life. I didn't find a single piece until that special walk back along the water's edge at low tide, where you infrequently find beach glass. There, in that special place I found half a dozen pieces. I wasn't left empty. I think God was telling me to look within, in the place where I didn't expect to find what I needed, rather than without for comfort in the external — joy and happiness are always found within, even when they're not.

Yesterday, nothing. Today, a plethora of beach glass — both in quantity and in quality — numerous special pieces, large, dark blue and even red! There was no obvious difference in conditions to account for it. Clearly it was a reminder that what we seek is not available to us every day, and that just because we can't find it one time doesn't mean it isn't there for us. The beach glass I found today was there, somewhere, yesterday, just not available to me. Then, for reasons I may never know, it became available to me today.

Faith. Diligence. Perseverance.

*B*rown beach glass is virtually impossible to see against the sand. It is most often found when retrieving a piece of white or green beach glass. If you stay alert and open to the possibility, you may see the brown beach glass lying nearby. How like the truth this is — often unseen, often open to us when we're searching elsewhere, if we're alert to "seeing" something different than we are seeking.

When someone, admiring our collection of beach glass, wishes they could have collected it, I think of Vladimir Horowitz's line (at least I think it was his) when someone gushed at him, "I'd give anything to play like you do" he replied, "no you wouldn't, you wouldn't practice eight hours a day like I do." I wonder how many people would be willing to spend time each and every day searching for beach glass, some days coming home with nothing, other times with a few pieces and occasionally (only occasionally) dozens. But truth or God are rarely found in one burst of bright white light. They are most often found in the minutiae of day to day living and seeking over time. It's a little like the Zen saying that if you meet the Buddha along the road in your meditation, kill Him.

*Some mornings I am consciously unconscious
— if that's possible — surrounded with a thick
fog even though the sun may be shining brightly.
I look for beach glass, not even aware of what
I've found, but certain that it serves me
in ways I cannot see.* 🐚

*W*hen you find one truth, stay alert and focused. Additional truths are often found nearby. At least that is the way it sometimes is with beach glass. This morning, on the wide expanse of broad, bright beach, all the glass that I found, about a dozen pieces, was all found in one relatively small area. Maybe that was just to remind me of and reinforce this truth.

When word of all this beach glass gathering gets out I'm quite certain the government will want to regulate it. I mean, if you don't protect beach glass you never know what could happen to it. Mandatory quotas will no doubt be imposed. Maybe I can get a subsidy for not picking up beach glass — so much per piece not collected. I'm quite certain the government knows God's intentions for beach glass a lot better than one lone searcher!

*S*haring my morning search for beach glass with a very good friend is a joyful experience, especially watching how quickly they are seduced by a process they may never have considered. But, the sharing doesn't allow the same level of introspection or deepening. Ultimately we each have to find our own path to God. It's like trying to walk in another person's footsteps in the snow — exhausting, in fact nearly impossible. Yet many footsteps can lay down a broad path to point us in one direction. But, we must make our own footsteps, our own path to the God that is within each of us. What is your beach glass?

I have lost count of the number of times I have bent
down to retrieve a very small, insignificant piece of
beach glass — almost too small to be retrieved —
and found a large piece of beach glass. Logically you
would expect it to be the other way around — the
large piece would bring you close to and therefore
reveal the small. Then I realized that the path to
a large truth, to God, is made up of a vast array of
small, seemingly insignificant truths
that are very hard to pick up.

Why retrieve the small piece of beach glass? I have never forgotten the lesson taught to me by a dear friend who had made a revolutionary change in his life that put him in a place diametrically opposed to where he had been. I asked him how one made the decision to make such a change and he advised me that you could not make such a decision. You made a lot of little, seemingly minor decisions.

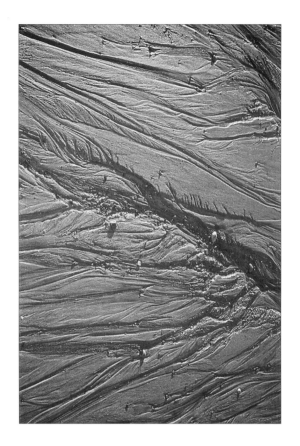

Beach Glass is a great teacher of the concept "Be Here Now."
When beach glass is plentiful on the beach it demands the time it
takes to gather it, for what else can be more important than
responding to the gifts the universe is bestowing on you —
gifts that won't be there "next time." There may be a great deal of
beach glass again but it won't be the same beach glass. This beach
glass, this day, is either gathered or the universe takes it back to
decide when and if to bring it forward again. How many things
in our life are exactly the same, and just how important is
that thing that is taking us from them?

*T*his morning I was late for work as a result of the
plenitude of beach glass that I was gifted with by the
universe. What could I have missed in being late to
the office that will last longer than the beach glass
collected, or the truths learned, or the seeds planted
for truths to be learned. Tomorrow, when beach glass
is scant, I can be early. 🐚

A few days of abundance can fill containers left empty during weeks of scarcity.

After a while, days of plenty create a concern that you are not worthy of the abundance and/or it foreshadows a decline. At least it creates that concern if you were raised Irish Catholic. But, one must see in the days of plenty the days of scarcity and recognize them as the same. Then, and this is the harder part, see in the days of scarcity the days of plenty and realize that those days bring the same level of God's love, grace and abundance. I don't suggest this as a visualization of creating ("I am the creator of my own universe") but rather as a recognition of the essential truth that God's love is ever-present and is not tied to quantity or to a specific gift. Camus was expressing exactly this thought (and probably a great deal more as well) when he said: "The struggle itself toward the heights is enough to fill a man's heart. One must imagine Sisyphus happy." Or, to say it less eloquently, one must imagine Sisyphus saying "Oh boy, I get to push the rock back up the hill again, my journey is not over, the opportunity to grow towards God not yet over. Life continues." 🐚

*I*t only takes a few days of scarcity to make me eat some of
my words and to turn a beautiful metaphor into a rock!
The lesson: some lessons are learned only in times of scarcity and,
with benevolence, God will present us with the lessons we need to
learn (and relearn) if we are open to seeing them, right in front of us.
Obstacles and guardians to the lessons may be put in our path, but
diligence, perseverance and commitment will allow us access
to the lessons — most of the time. 🐚

In California I collected beach glass. If I add it to a jar of the beach glass collected in Massachusetts you couldn't pick out the California glass — it would look the same. You might assume the Atlantic and the Pacific are the same because they are two oceans and yet the differences are as numerous as the similarities. I could pick out the California beach glass because for me, it's not just beach glass, it's a touchstone to the time spent walking that particular beach with a dear friend. And, that beach glass carries with it the reminder of his stories of life growing up on Crystal Cove Beach — and it always will. One more example of the profane made sacred. 🐚

There is a seemingly endless universe to view when walking on the beach at sunrise. I'm focused on the ground immediately beneath me searching for beach glass. It is through this "narrower" and more limited focus, this doorway to the infinite, that I am opening to a universe vastly larger than that which can be seen walking on the beach at sunrise.

My last morning on the beach before an extended absence.
*Sunrise and high tide coincided so I walked on that part of the beach
where you virtually never find beach glass, only to be gifted with
dozens of pieces — the first time such bounty has been bestowed
upon me on this section of beach. Perhaps the beach is
acknowledging me and reminding me to return, and in that
acknowledgment I am aware that the beach and ocean
that are making beach glass need the searcher for beach glass
in order to be.*

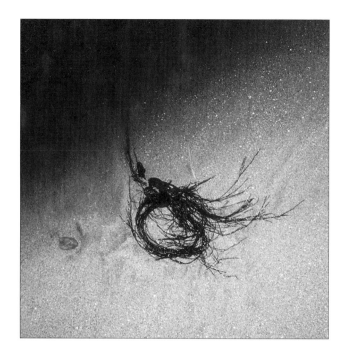

After returning to the beach from an absence I was gifted with a number of large pieces during my twilight walk that evening at low tide — I couldn't have seen smaller pieces in the fading sun so the beach provided what was needed. The next morning, the beach ran me through most of the lessons recounted above (far too many to repeat here), reminding me of and reinforcing what had been taught. And, I presume, verifying that the foundation was in place for the lessons that were to follow.

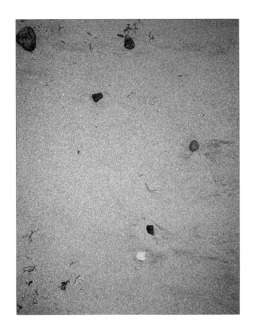

*T*his morning, a bright Spring day, I was profoundly
struck by how little what I was doing had to do with
beach glass. The beach glass was and is merely a
doorway to something much larger, fundamental to
our being, and profound beyond these words.
Of course, as I've said, that realization is much
easier with full pockets, as were mine this morning.
The saints could get there regardless of whether their
pockets were full or empty. The rest of us require a
doorway or a well worn path to point us in the
direction and guide us in our journey, reminding us
to give thanks to those who went before.

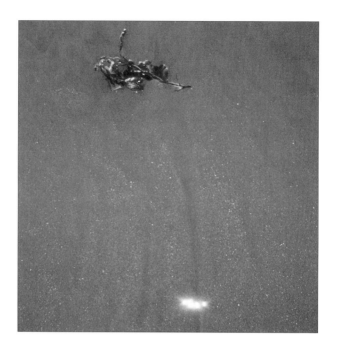

This morning I rose early to be on the beach at sunrise prior to a two week trip that would take me far from the ocean.

I was gifted with a huge quantity of beach glass (pockets literally overflowing), including three rare blue pieces (it had been weeks since I found a piece of blue). The first dozen pieces I gathered were all tear shaped (no hyperbole or metaphor here, we're talking distinctly tear shaped) as well as the last which was a very large and unusually thick piece. Now I know this must be coincidence, it has to be, but even so I'll carry the last piece with me on my journey as a touchstone back to this moment that so deeply and profoundly touched my heart (grabbed and squeezed it would be more accurate but less poetic). 🐚

What hat will I do if customs questions me on the value
of this large piece of beach glass I carry with me.
I can explain to them that there is no price that can
be put on it, that it is a touchstone into something so
profound and central to our being that it can't even
be expressed in words — at least not in my words,
I'm not that good. I mean how do you list this thing
on a customs declaration form? How do we speak
of God in a time that has forgotten how to speak to
God or to recognize God's presence in a piece of
beach glass.

*W*hile in Paris I didn't find beach glass but I did find the Nymphéas of Claude Monet at the Musée de l'Orangerie in which Monet transformed a pond of water lilies to something far beyond. Through vision blurred by the emotion of Monet's gift to me in that moment I saw ordinary beach glass transformed into jewels of unimaginable wealth and a universe in the finite.

In Dresden I watched the Symphony Orchestra play Strauss as the conductor molded himself to each note and ultimately became one with the music. It was then I realized that each of those notes, each crescendo was his beach glass and I felt a deep connection to his prayer. 🐚

*O*nce I can walk on the beach, I know I am truly home —
in heart and soul as well as body. This morning, in the first light
before sunrise I was rewarded and taught. On the first part of the
beach which usually offers scarcity there was abundance.
Then, as thoughts of overflowing pockets danced in my head,
on the part of the beach that normally offers abundance — scarcity,
letting me know to be in the moment, not to anticipate and to
celebrate what is already given me. On the walk back along the
water's edge, the sunrise exploded with the most brilliant gold color
to light the shoreline that I have ever seen. I not only felt "home,"
I also felt caressed and blessed.

I *put the blue piece of glass I found today*
in the middle of the pile of beach glass
I left next to the sink for my wife so that
she, too, could have the joy
of "discovering" it.

*O*n mornings when there is less beach glass to be found, you have
the opportunity to spend more time enjoying and coming to know
each piece that you do find. Even if you return home with lighter
pockets than the previous day, your heart is no less full,
your spirit no less enriched, and you've learned
another lesson that can serve you in life.

This *morning, with high tide asserting itself, I walked to the portion*
of the beach that is devoid of beach glass but rich in rocks that are
ideal for polishing. The bounty of rocks far exceeded the norm and
as I struggled home I realized a profound truth that escaped my
conscious mind prior to today: rocks are one hell of a lot heavier
than beach glass and overflowing pockets of rocks means something
very different from overflowing pockets of beach glass. Before you
scoff at my previous ignorance to this truth, ponder how many
obvious truths go unobserved in our lives.

*A*t the end of a sunrise walk on the beach

that offers the best rocks for polishing

I found one lone piece of beach glass,

resplendent and unique in its solitariness.

It served as yet another reminder that

we receive what we need even when

it is not expected or likely.

If I see a piece of beach glass I celebrate the moment and pick it up — every piece — well, not brand new glass that has not achieved the status of beach glass. I realized this morning, walking on the beach without beach glass that picking up rocks requires choice and selection — discernment in regards to suitability/desirability for polishing. I also realized that my choices were different morning to morning, week to week, when I began collecting rocks vs. now . . . It gives me pause to be less myopic about past choices and more open to what is in front of me now and what may be present to me tomorrow. In all this realizing, a quote from Nikos Kazantzakis framed on my wall at the office and at home deepened and opened more fully for me:

"Die every day.
Be born every day.
Deny everything everyday.
The superior virtue is not to be
free but to fight for freedom." 🐚

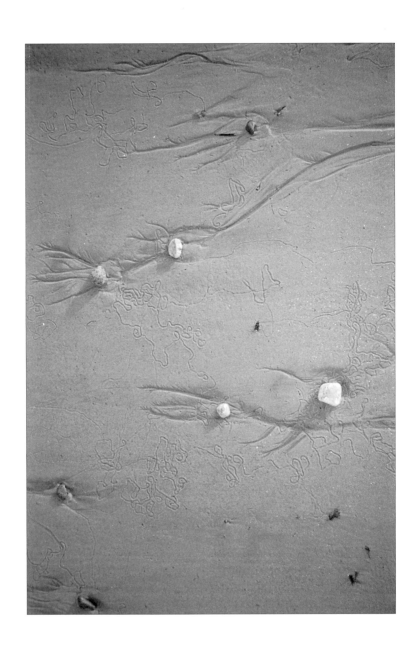

Note on a fog caressed beach coated with an ever so thin covering of Spring rain: a rock has to be spectacular to be picked up once my pockets are overflowing and walking has become weight training. It challenges me to see beyond my own personal fog and to wonder about all that I have passed up in my life because I did not consider letting go of something I already had and, how many times I will do that today and in the future. See the previous Nikos Kazantzakis quote for a more eloquent elaboration of this point.

A decided chill in the air with a distinctive bite to the wind. I walked the beach engrossed in some mundane matter that seemed like life and death. And in a moment, unexpectedly, I was warmed. I turned to see that the sun had burst through and was hurtling spikes of brilliant light through the clouds. I realized that I was warmed from the inside as well as the outside. Surely this gift was more than an accident of creation and the symmetry of a biological entity with a physical one. Offer what explanation you will, I left the beach in a joyful place, feeling touched by the hand of God. This was not a moment for theology. 🐚

*T*his morning, fog bound both internally and externally, I found just one solitary piece of beach glass on the entire expanse of beach.

It was a fairly large piece, unique in its shape and spectacular in its overall design. It was enough to reconnect me to God this morning and for that I am very grateful. 🐚

*A*bundance, following a prolonged period
of scarcity brings with it a special joy and Grace.
This morning, I was more appreciative of the
Grace than the abundance, knowing that
in that Grace is the greater gift.

This morning, Grace came not in abundance but in quality —
the quality of the early morning light, the sun rising and the moon
setting at opposite ends of the beach, the ocean as calm as a country
lake with a curl to its lip at the edge, and, each piece of beach glass
found was of a unique and special color or shape, faceted to catch
the morning light and reflect it deep inside. A person could choose
not to believe in God this morning but it wouldn't be easy —
they would have to believe in something greater than themselves.
Grace has a way of doing that. 🐚

In the Summer months, sand covers the rocks and the beach glass that accompanies them, much to the delight of the kids and families out for a day's outing. I continue to look for beach glass in spite of the fact that it is rarely there. The opportunity: to learn the value of looking, unobstructed by finding. 🐚

In Summer and early Fall the sand creates a pristine beach. Underneath the pristine remains the plenitude of rocks and the never ending supply of beach glass that will be brought forth once again come late Fall or Winter. This seemingly picture perfect, smooth and uninterrupted beach helps me to fully absorb Heinrich Zimmer's quote from The King and the Corpse: "The obvious is only the semblance; beneath lies something hidden, the real. And whoever clings only to the semblance will become entangled in it before he knows." And, it also challenges me to look beyond the prejudices and limitations I've placed on God. Inviting and enjoyable as the beach might be, it is what is underneath that is feeding my soul.

In these days of not finding I keep looking. Why? The search is not in what has been found but in what has yet to be found and in the looking. William S. Burroughs in writing why he was not concerned about not yet knowing "the answer" said: "All is in the not yet done." And, in the Tao of Beach Glass all is in the search and the beach glass not yet found. In that realization is joy.

*I am quite certain that in spite of our certainty
that the sun will rise there is deep within us,
somewhere, a sense of relief when it actually
does, deep in that place that constantly
celebrates the Grace of life. That is the feeling
these last few days as the sand returned the rocks
and the beach glass to the beach without fanfare,
without notice but with certainty,
as I knew it would.*